OUR WORLD OF MYSTERIES

Fascinating Facts About the Planet Earth

By Suzanne Lord

SCHOLASTIC INC.
New York Toronto London Auckland Sydney

To the most important parts of my world:
Family, Friends, Music, and Writing

Photo Credits

Page 6: Animals, Animals. Page 16: Frans Lanting. Page 24: AP/Wide World. Page 29: Leonard Von Matt/Photo Researchers. Page 35: Scala Fine Arts. Page 39: AP/Wide World. Page 42: George Holton/Photo Researchers. Page 48: AP/Wide World. Page 53: Illustration by George Retseck from "The Supercontinent Cycle," by R. Damian Nance, Thomas R. Worsley, and Judith B. Moody. July 1988. Page 60: C. J. Collins/Photo Researchers. Page 64: AP/Wide World. Page 68: Tom McHugh/Photo Researcher. Page 70: Tom McHugh/Photo Researcher. Page 77: Tom McHugh/Photo Researcher. Page 80: Tom McHugh/Photo Researcher. Page 83: Sovfoto. Page 85: AP/Wide World.

ISBN 0-590-44595-2

Copyright © 1991 by Suzanne Lord. All rights reserved. Published by Scholastic Inc.

12 11 10 9 8 7 6 5 4 3 2 1   1 2 3 4 5 6/9

Printed in the U.S.A.   28

First Scholastic printing, September 1991

Contents

Introduction

The earth has more mysteries than a library full of Sherlock Holmes stories. Why did dinosaurs disappear from the face of the earth? What kind of creatures live only in darkness? Who were the Marajoara and what were their lives like? Where is the wettest place on the earth? When did fish swim in what is now desert land?

Through the chapters of this book, you will find that our world is not the familiar place it once seemed. Instead, it is an adventure that humans have hardly begun to explore.

Join that adventure and journey with us now, into the unfamiliar and unknown territory that we call Earth.

1
Unearthly Places on Earth

You don't have to be an astronaut to explore strange new worlds. There are places right here on Earth that look like something a science fiction writer might dream up!

At our North and South poles, for instance, are areas of unbelievable cold where the ice never melts. In other places, volcanic eruptions have left piles of once-liquid lava (melted rock) that have cooled and hardened into rivers of stone. There are also desert areas where miles of sand resemble waves of water where true rain seldom falls.

But what about strange, alienlike life forms? There are plenty of those on Earth, too! Mayflies, small flying gnatlike insects, have an entire lifespan of one day, while some Sequoia trees are over 2,000 years old. Whales huge enough to swallow rowboats live on organisms too small to see with the naked eye, and sing songs of haunting beauty. Frogs spend their early life underwater and their later years as air-breathers.

But even faced with so many places and life forms, a few stand out as extra-weird. Here are four of them.

Caves: Life Without Light

Caves have three main divisions: the entrance, a "twilight" area, and the interior. A cave entrance provides shelter for a number of "visitors," including humans. The twilight area holds animals that live inside the cave, but that still hunt outside the cave. Bats are twilight area animals. Their droppings and their dead bodies fall to the bottom of the twilight cave area and serve as food for other animals, such as cave beetles. Fungi, nonflowering parasitic plants, also grow in the twilight area.

Deep inside caves, however, life is quite different. There is absolutely no light, *ever*, in a cave interior. And a cave interior is so far away from seasonal changes outside that the temperature always stays the same. (Usually interior cave temperatures hover around 50 degrees Fahrenheit.) It is also always damp. Humidity is 100 percent!

Cave interior animals live in streams that flow through the cave system. There are fish, worms, beetles, a type of crayfish, millipedes, salamanders, and even some shrimp. This sounds like a lot of animal life, but actually only a few animals can live in a cave interior at any one time, because food is so scarce.

These animals have several things in common. They are smaller than their outside relatives, since there isn't enough food in a cave interior to support a really large animal. Cave interior animals are blind. Because they live in total darkness, they have no need for eyes. Some have what used to be eyes, underneath eyelids that have grown together. Others have nothing at all where eyes should be.

Also, because there is no light where they live, these animals have no need for skin color. Actually, they look like they are light pink. But this isn't real "color." The animals' skin is transparent. The pink color comes from their blood showing through their skin!

Since there is no light, no plants can grow. So what do animals in a cave interior eat? The answer is — anything they can find! Periodic floods wash plant and animal matter in from outside the cave. Sometimes non-cave animals wander too far into a cave, get lost, and die in the interior. They then become food. Even if these animals find their way out, they sometimes leave droppings which can also become food. Often, bat droppings (called guano) fall into cave springs, are carried into the cave's interior, and become food. And, finally, interior cave dwellers will also eat one another!

If you think all caves are alike — think again! Different types of interior cave animals live in different areas of the world. Caves in Kentucky,

Texas, Oklahoma, and in the Ozark mountains of America contain white, blind salamanders. A huge version of these salamanders, called *Proteus*, is found in Yugoslavian caves. These "giants" can grow up to a foot in length.

Many Florida caves are known for their strange-looking crayfish. These creatures are colorless and eyeless! According to Horton Hobbs, a scientist who has made a lifetime study of them, there are two types of these crayfish. One is a tiny 1¼" variety that hangs from cave ceilings, and is so light that it can walk on water scum without sinking! The other is a 3–4" variety that lives on the bottom of cave pools. Both types live in the same place, since they don't occupy the same areas or compete for food.

Before you start thinking that weird creatures live only in American caves, British caves have ½" to ¾" transparent, blind shrimp in their shallow interior pools. As cave explorer Tony Waltham described, "Its whole blood system is visible as it swims around in its own little world."

American and Mexican caves contain many blindfish. These fish are a great curiosity for tourists. But they are very small, and not what most people think they're going to see.

One cave owner collected blindfish and kept them in a display pool for tourists to look at. But everyone looked at the tiny fish and thought they were just ordinary minnows. "So," the owner said,

"I tossed a thirty-pound white catfish into that pool. As far as I know, that catfish could see like an eagle. I didn't even say it was nearsighted. But everybody looked at it and said 'See that big blind fish' and went away happy!"

The Ocean Abyss: More Life Without Light

Like caves, oceans also have three areas. Most of the ocean life that we are familiar with comes from the top third, which is closest to the surface. The middle ocean depth is dark, cold, under a lot of pressure, and holds most of the "bioluminescent" ocean life. In other words, many mid-depth life-forms glow in the dark. One of the most famous is the anglerfish. This fish has a "fishing rod" grow-

A closeup shot of an anglerfish.

ing out of its forehead, with a glowing "lure" at the end of it. In the ocean darkness, only the lure is visible. Anything that gets close enough to try to eat the lure finds that it is also close enough to become an anglerfish dinner!

Scientists used to think that mid-depth life-forms were from the ocean abyss. But that was before we realized how *really* deep oceans are. The ocean abyss is between 3,000 and 5,000 meters deep. That's approximately 10,000 feet to 16,500 feet below the surface. To get an idea of how deep that is, the Matterhorn Mountain in the Swiss Alps is 14,690 feet up! There are areas of the ocean that are even deeper, but they have not been explored yet.

No human can dive to the true bottom of the ocean unaided. Think of how your head feels when you swim in the bottom of the deep end of a swimming pool. It feels like the water is pushing against you, right? Well, it is. This is water pressure, and it gets more and more intense as the water gets deeper. If humans dived too deeply into the ocean their bones would snap under the pressure. Even diving suits can only get humans into mid-ocean range.

Only a few people have seen the ocean abyss. One group crammed into a tiny, extremely sturdy "ship," which was stocked with cameras and scientific equipment. The ship was carried most of the way to the bottom of the ocean by submarine.

Then it was lowered to the ocean floor and left. After a day of study, the ship was hauled back to the submarine and taken topside again.

Like a cave interior, there is absolutely no light at the bottom of the ocean abyss. And so, once again, there are no plants at all. Every animal in the abyss is either a scavenger living on what floats to the ocean floor, or a carnivore eating other animals. Food of any kind is scarce.

Even though all abyssal life is animal, many creatures look like plants. In fact, one main life form is known as a sea cucumber. This animal is shaped like a fat cuke covered with short, spiny tentacles. One scientist described them as "small tumbleweeds rolling on the ocean floor."

One of the more fascinating animals living in the ocean abyss is the abyssal tube worm. These worms live inside a casing that looks like plastic. When they feel safe, the worms let their feeding tentacles flow out of the tube to wave in the current and pick up any food floating by. "They look," an observer has said, "for all the world like small feather dusters." But when disturbed, the "feather duster" tentacles duck back into the protection of their casing, and then the tube worms look like ballpoint pens stuck into the ocean bottom!

Another "star" of the ocean abyss is the starfish. Several types live on the deep ocean floor. Some resemble the starfish that we are used to seeing. But most are brittle stars, with long raylike arms.

They row themselves along the ocean floor with two arms on either side, and eat whatever they find on the bottom.

Something starfish eat a lot of are molluscs, such as clams. These, too, live in the abyss, but scientists don't see them because molluscs bury themselves in the sand! Many types of sea worms do the same, and are also very rarely seen.

The ocean bottom is home to a distinctive-looking octopus. This animal has tentacles like the more familiar surface octopus, but the tentacles are connected by webbing. When lying on the bottom, the abyssal octopus looks like an open umbrella.

Sea urchins are the "cows" of the abyss. They move slowly along the ocean bottom and "graze" on ooze and clay. For this reason they're known as "the vacuum cleaners of the ocean."

Several types of fish live in the abyss. They range in size from tiny slivers to three-foot monsters. The most common is called the rat-tail fish. It has a large head, and a long, tapering tail. Although it has large eyes, lights seem to have no effect on it. Scientists have no proof, but feel that the fish is probably blind.

Other fish are bottom feeders, built with a long snout over a short jaw. This way they can poke around in the ooze, looking for dinner among the animals that live on the bottom.

One abyssal fish is called the tripod fish. That's

because it stands on two long, spiny fins facing the current, apparently feeding on whatever floats by. Scientists don't know too much about them, because no one has ever seen a tripod fish move! "If its fins had not been moving slightly [in the ocean current]," one scientist said, "I would have believed it stuffed!"

Few fish visit the abyss from above. Some sleeper sharks and dogfish have been seen in the abyss. Scientists set out bait to lure abyssal life into camera range, and these fish sometimes take the bait.

Only one mammal can dive into the abyss by itself — the sperm whale. Unfortunately, these whales sometimes become entangled in deep-sea communication cables. We know this because when workers bring up cables from the abyss for repairs, they also get a rotting whale carcass. The cable wraps around their jaws or their tail or a flipper, and traps them. Since whales are air-breathers, they drown.

Just as in cave life, it sounds like there is a lot of life on the ocean bottom. That's not true. These life forms are widely scattered. Descriptions of their many forms are the result of years of study.

Many abyssal animals haven't been discovered yet. And scientists can't figure out how others live. Tiny threadlike "bread-bearers," for instance, have no visible means of feeding. And yet they're obviously alive!

Studying abyssal life is frustrating. As one scientist said, "You can't swim around with a net catching things." Mechanical arms don't move fast enough to catch swiftly moving organisms. And, even if scientists could catch abyssal animals, they couldn't bring them to the surface for study. Just as we would be crushed by ocean pressure if we dived into the abyss, abyssal animals would explode from the *lack* of pressure if they were brought to the ocean's surface!

The Driest Place on Earth:
The Atacama Desert

The Atacama Desert is located in the South American countries of Chile and Peru. It is the smallest major desert in the world — 140,000 square miles. But it has the least moisture of any area on the earth; so little, in fact, that it is not measurable!

Ironically, the Atacama Desert's western border is the Pacific Ocean! But a combination of winds and a north-south mountain range keep ocean moisture from traveling inland. The very edge of the Atacama has a misty fog from which a few hardy plants can squeeze enough moisture to live on. Unfortunately, the mist does not contain enough moisture to condense into rain. And what little moisture there is, is blown away by ocean winds.

Unlike most deserts, the Atacama is not hot.

Cold ocean currents keep the air cool, even though it is not moist.

The very edge of the Atacama Desert supports some meager animal life. The Peruvian fox lives on the coastland, where it eats dead fish, crabs, and even seaweed. In winter it moves into the mountains where it becomes a temporary vegetarian, living on seeds and shrubs!

Beyond the coast, however, are areas so unbelievably bare it might as well be Mars. Yet people live in these areas, and some have become fabulously wealthy.

Mining operations have brought humans where no plant or animal can live. Ironically, the place where nothing grows is one of the world's greatest sources of nitrate — the world's best fertilizer.

Millions of years ago, the Atacama Desert was part of the ocean floor. When it rose above the ocean and dried out, all the oceanic minerals were left. Since it never rained, none of these deposits was washed away. If the present Atacama soil were watered, it would be some of the richest farmland on Earth!

This irony is not lost on scientists. "The Atacama Desert," wrote one scientist, "one of the richest zones on Earth, produces nothing to eat. Not a bulb, a leaf, or a blade of grass; scarcely an animal or bird can live there. Man's life, where he digs out Earth's best fertilizer, depends upon food shipped in from poorer lands. It is like a fable of starving to death on a mountain of gold."

Besides nitrates, the Atacama is also mined for salt, gypsum, borax, and phosphates.

The Atacama Desert interior is a sight few travelers forget. Even from the air, it looks burned out. "From an automobile, we saw . . . only brown-black desert: not dusty, not sandy, just degenerate rock heavily weighing down the earth." The traveler who wrote this account saw only one plant all day — a spindly pepper tree living on the drip from a railroad water tower.

One river, the Loa, flows through the Atacama. Along this river are the only towns possible. Old maps show other rivers crossing the area. And there are artifacts from an ancient civilization — the Atacameños—who once lived there.

The Atacameños' civilization flourished over 2,000 years ago, and lasted hundreds of years. They fished, bred llamas to sell to other tribes, and grew crops. Archaeologists say the desert was not as dry in those days. In some parts of the desert edge "whole forests have been discovered buried under the sand." Perhaps their land was slowly eaten up by the desert, as lands in Africa are today.

The Wettest Place on Earth: Mount Waialeale

Mount Waialeale (pronounced: Why-ollie-OLL-ie) is located on the island of Kauai in Hawaii. In fact it is in the center of Kauai, and its ancient volcanic action is the reason that the island is there in the first place.

Waialeale means "rippling water" in Hawaiian. It's a very fitting name. Moisture-filled ocean winds are blown up the sides of the mountain. At the top of the mountain, all the moisture condenses and rains down. This constant activity has made Mount Waialeale the wettest place on Earth. *Average* rainfall is 480″ per year! One year the annual rainfall measured 624″!

Not very many people visit the mountain because it is surrounded by an almost impassable swamp. This has made Mount Waialeale a place of legends, of superstitions, and of mystery.

Mount Waialeale is rumored to be the hiding place of the last of the "menehune" (many-HEW-nee). Descriptions of the menehune sound very much like descriptions of leprechauns to outsiders. They were a small, light-skinned race, who were fabulous carvers of stone. They once were the only people on the island of Kauai. But when the larger Polynesians arrived, the menehunes were taken over and became servants.

When Europeans arrived, the menehune left. One day they were around, and the next day they were not! Superstition dictates that the last surviving menehunes live quietly out of sight in the wilderness of Waialeale.

Besides possible menehunes, Mount Waialeale contains other forms of life not found anywhere else. These life forms are plants and birds. There are no native mammals there, and surprisingly, no reptiles or amphibious life at all.

Still, despite the lack of snakes and the abundance of rare plants, scientists have been slow to study Waialeale's life-forms. "The reason is," one botanist said, "I want to live!"

People have entered the Alakai swamp surrounding Mount Waialeale and never returned. "The turf covering the quagmire," wrote one hardy visitor, "would tremble for yards in every direction at every step. Too often, it would give way, plunging us hip-deep in mire."

In the 1950s, developers tried to build a road through the Alakai swamp and into Mount Waialeale. Rain prevented the bulldozer from getting more than a few yards into the thick forest. The next day, workers couldn't find the bulldozer. It hadn't been stolen. It had sunk! No one has tried to develop the area since then.

One botanist, Michael Doyle, has been risking life and limb to study the largest herb in the world, which grows in the Alakai swamp beside Mt. Waialeale. The herb is called "ape ape" (AH-pay AH-pay). Scientists know it as gunnera. Its leaves are 8 feet wide. Humans look like midgets standing near gunnera.

Gunnera is older than the dinosaurs. It has no known living relatives. It is the same now as fossils that date back 95 *million* years!

What is it like to walk around the wettest spot on Earth? "Everything was green," Doyle said.

15

"The light was green. It was all amazingly beautiful — unless you tried to move."

A patch of land that looks as even as a golf course might actually be hiding a deep hole. Once, Doyle stepped onto what looked like solid ground and ended up dangling upside down off a cliff instead! Also, it's easy to get lost. Doyle left markers in the swamp, telling him which way he should travel to get to the edge. But even with these, he once was so lost that he thought he might never find his way out again!

Michael Doyle with a gunnera plant at Mount Waialeale.

2
Vanishing Peoples

Anyone who has ever moved into a house after someone else has lived in it knows what it's like to wonder about vanishing peoples. The new people find little things, like a stray comb, and wonder about the former occupants. Were they nice? Did they have kids? Pets? Would you like to have known them?

The world is a bit like an enormous old house. We are the new occupants. Plenty of folks have lived here before us. Sometimes we find things from the former occupants. We didn't know them, but we wonder about them. What were they like?

Some civilizations, such as the Romans, Greeks, and Chinese, left a lot behind to tell us about them. Others did not. In fact, some civilizations vanished so completely that they were forgotten for hundreds of years. The Mayan civilization is like that.

Once Mayans dominated what is now Mexico and Guatemala. They lived in large cities full of carefully constructed buildings. Some of the buildings were several stories high. They had a complicated written language that used over 850 pictures instead of letters. Mayans watched the movements of planets and stars carefully. Their calendar was as accurate as the one we use today! Their religion, system of government, and social system seem to have been very complicated and highly sophisticated. They were a vital, intelligent, thriving culture. Then they disappeared.

No one knows exactly what happened to make the Mayans abandon their major cities. But Mayans who lived in other cities fought among themselves for power. Then the Spanish arrived and conquered the remaining Mayans in many battles during the 1500s. The Mayan language was lost. Their religion was forgotten.

But stories remained of fabulous cities lost in Central American jungles. Explorers came and found, covered in jungle growth, the abandoned cities of the Mayans. The many artifacts recovered from these ancient cities have made Mayan art famous throughout the world.

Scientists still do not know how to read the Mayan language. We only know what we can tell from their stone carvings. Mayans remain one of the world's most famous Vanishing Peoples.

The Ban Chiang of Thailand
When the world thinks of ancient Oriental cul-

tures, we think of China or Japan or even India. Places like Thailand, Cambodia, and Laos in Southeast Asia, had ancient cultures, too. But until recently they haven't been considered important. Also, these areas have often been at war in this century, which has hampered study!

Scientists assumed that ancient Thai cultures were made up of simple hunter-gatherers, who didn't do much, have much of a society, or make anything of beauty or value. But all that was before one maverick Western archaeologist, Chester Gorman, began studying Thailand in the 1970s. After investigating several promising sites, Gorman soon homed in on an area in northeastern Thailand called Ban Chiang. In 1974, Gorman and a Thai Fine Arts professor named Charoenwongsa hit pay dirt. They found an area that had been lived in for 6,000 years. One city was built on top of another. The farther down they dug, the older things got.

Gorman and Charoenwongsa didn't find just a few artifacts. Right away, they came up with 18 *tons* of material. There were 123 burial sites. There were hundreds of bronze tools, weapons, and pieces of jewelry. And there were over a million pieces of broken pottery.

The good news is that Gorman and Charoenwongsa had found evidence of a thriving Bronze-Age culture. This is an ancient culture that on a regular basis used metal for their tools and weapons. Since bronze is the metal most commonly used, such cultures are known as Bronze Age. No one had suspected that ancient peoples in Southeast Asia had gone through this stage of cultural development.

The bad news is that the culture had no written language, and the pottery designs do not have scenes of daily life on them. We don't even know what these people called themselves. Right now, they are known as the Ban Chiang because that is the region where their remains were found.

But we do know that they were very skilled in metalworking. They knew how to mix different types of metals for different purposes. Some Ban Chiang metals had to be heated to at least 1,000 degrees Fahrenheit to have been made at all!

From the millions of pottery shards found, some pieces of pottery have been put back together. The pots are beautifully made and highly decorated. There is no one "tribal style" either. The designs are very different from one pot to another.

No one knows what happened to the ancient Ban Chiang. They seem to have simply vanished. But now scientists wonder if other vanished civilizations are waiting to be found in Southeast Asia! It is a territory, one scientist said, "waiting to be excavated."

The Marajoara

The Amazon is the second longest river in the world. It flows over South America from west to east, mainly across Brazil. The river is so long that it almost cuts the top quarter of South America off from the rest! It carries more water than any other river through some of the most inhospitable jungle land in the world until it ends in the Atlantic Ocean.

Land surrounding the Amazon River is largely uninhabited. The only people seem to be scattered tribes of small, fierce Indians. They are sparse in number and, in the words of one encyclopedia, "of meager cultural material." Scientists have felt until recently that the Amazon area has always been made up of these primitive, semi-nomadic tribes.

Then in 1983, both North and South American scientists explored an area of the Amazon not studied before. To their own surprise, they found ancient remains of highly developed, settled farming communities with hundreds of thousands of people.

Just as with the Ban Chiang, we do not know what these people called themselves. But since their ancient cities were found in the Marajó region of Amazonia, they are known as the Marajoara.

The Marajoara lived in an area that flooded periodically. But instead of building their houses on stilts, as some people have, they built entire "islands" to live on! These are not little hills, either. Most mounds are ten to twenty feet higher than the surrounding ground — and 6 or 7 *acres* in area!

The tallest mound found so far is 65 feet high! The one with the largest area is over 50 acres!

On the mounds, Marajoara built communal dwellings. Each family had its own clay baking hearth. The average dwelling had nine of these. Figuring four people per family, each place would house about 36 people. Each mound had from five to ten (or more) dwellings on it, meaning that several hundred people lived on each "island." By counting this way, scientists have figured that the Marajoara people numbered at least 100,000 at any one time! Some mounds had people living on them continuously, for hundreds of years.

Marajoara lived very differently than Amazon tribes today. They were settled, and grew crops. These crops were stored so that there was enough food throughout the year, without periods of famine. They were a clean people with well-defined garbage dumps. Unlike Amazon tribes today, they did not seem to eat many fish.

Marajoara looked different from present-day Amazon Indians. How do we know? Scientists found Marajoara dead inside burial urns. These were 2-foot to 3-foot tall pots, with the corpses tightly flexed inside. When examined, the bodies were of a taller people, strong and well-nourished.

Marajoara were very artistic people. They made a wide variety of tools and pottery, and decorated everything. They even painted the bones of some of their dead, although nobody is sure why.

Scientists know more about what the Marajoara looked like than they do about the Ban Chiang, because Marajoara art shows people. There are people painted on funerary urns and pots. There are statues, small figurines, and even musical instruments in the shape of Marajoara people.

Scientists were impressed by the beautifully decorated tunics that Marajoara wore. The shape of these tunics looks like the ones worn by some present-day South American Indians.

The Marajoara disappeared around 1300 A.D., before any Europeans came to the Americas. What happened to them? Where did they go? As one scientist said, "the fate of the long-lived Marajoara culture itself remains a mystery."

The Anasazi

A thousand years ago, thriving communities of Native Americans made their homes in what is now Colorado, New Mexico, Arizona, and southern Utah. The homes are still there. The people disappeared. Once again, we don't know what these people called themselves. But Native Americans of today call them "the old ones" — Anasazi.

The Anasazi must have been an amazing people. Resourceful and intelligent, they carved entire cities into the sides of high cliffs. Sometimes they built their cities on the flat tops of "mesas," a type of desert mountain. Some of these areas have been declared national parks. The most famous Anasazi

Cliff dwellings in Mesa Verde National Park, Colorado.

"cliff dwellings" are in the Mesa Verde Colorado National Park.

The Anasazi had a vast system of roads that has only recently been discovered, thanks to infrared photographs taken from jets. This road system meant that different Anasazi cities were in contact and that they may have traded goods with one another.

Infrared photography has also shown how resourceful the Anasazi were in another way. The Anasazi farmed in one of the most arid (dry) areas of North America. Infrared photographs taken from jets showed 10-foot by 10-foot square areas that seemed to have a different temperature from surrounding soil. These squares were the Anasazis' garden plots hidden under the existing soil layers of today.

Scientists investigated these plots and found that the soil in those spots was mixed with hundreds of thousands of tiny pebbles. The pebbles helped keep moisture in the soil, and kept water from evaporating under the hot desert sun. They also collected heat during the day and kept the soil warm at night, when desert temperatures dropped drastically.

The Anasazi seem to have moved away from their homes about 500 years ago. Nobody knows why the Anasazi abandoned their cities and disappeared, but they did. Perhaps the area became too dry, even for their clever farming. Though the

Anasazi civilization was lost forever, some few who stayed may have sowed the seeds of other Native American civilizations. Both Pueblo and Navaho people believe that the Anasazi are their direct ancestors.

3
Lost — and Found?

In Chapter 2, we looked at civilizations that were lost and forgotten. But sometimes civilizations aren't forgotten, even though they *have* been lost. We call them legends — until someone finds them! The city of Pompeii is an example of a legendary place, once lost, and now found.

Two thousand years ago, Pompeii was a thriving, prosperous Roman port city. An ancient volcano, Mount Vesuvius, loomed over the inhabitants. But nobody was worried. Vesuvius had been inactive since beyond memory.

But in 79 A.D., Vesuvius rumbled, sending earthquake tremors throughout the city. Citizens were unnerved. Then the tremors stopped. People relaxed, thinking the danger was over. A few weeks later Pompeii had more, deeper tremors. Some people left, but the rest waited for Vesuvius to calm down.

A week after that, the tremors were accompanied by a strange blast of hot air. The sky went dark. Shocked citizens noticed that Vesuvius didn't look the same anymore. This time, the mountain had split open.

Suddenly Vesuvius began spitting out fiery ashes, poisonous smoke, burning stones, and a flood of boiling mud! People tried to run, but the darkness was so heavy that they could not see where they were headed. Pompeii's citizens panicked completely.

Some lucky people made it to Pompeii's harbor, grabbed a boat, and escaped. The rest died of injuries, were killed by poison gases, or were smothered in the tons of volcanic ash and mud that eventually buried the city completely. Pompeii was gone. In its place was a layer of thick mud and ash that soon dried to the hardness of cement.

Roman eyewitnesses and historians wrote about the end of Pompeii. So, for hundreds of years, people knew that there had once been a Roman city that was wiped out by a volcano's fury. But nobody knew exactly where to look for it. And even if they did, there were no tools strong enough to dig through the hard, 2,000-year-old layer of ash and mud. It wasn't until the twentieth century that archaeologists could locate Pompeii and begin digging it out.

In 1956, an archaeologist named Fiorelli noticed that there were many curious "hollow" spots in the ash. At the bottom of the holes, he would always find a few large bones. Curious, he filled a hole with plaster of paris. When the plaster dried, Fiorelli removed it. To his amazement, he had a complete body cast of a citizen of Pompeii — in the exact posture in which the person had died. The bodies themselves had long rotted, except for a few of the larger bones. But the ash and mud had preserved their exact shape for eternity.

These amazing plaster casts of actual ancient Romans spurred interest in Pompeii and other areas that had been destroyed by Mount Vesuvius. Slowly, over the last 30 years, Pompeii has been recovered. Once a lost, legendary city, Pompeii has now been found by a fascinated world.

Plaster models of bodies in Pompeii, Italy.

The Ancient City of Troy

Troy was the site of the Trojan war. This war was fought over 3,000 years ago between the Trojans and the ancient Greeks. We know about it because an ancient Greek named Homer made up a very long story about it, called the *Iliad*. This story was told from generation to generation. Finally it was written down.

For thousands of years, scholars studied Homer's *Iliad*, which told of the conquering and destruction of Troy. But no one knew whether there had really been a Trojan war. And if there had been, where was the ruined city of Troy?

During the late 1800s, scholars studied Homer's work carefully. Eventually they figured that the ancient city must have been in an area now part of the country of Turkey. From 1870 to 1890, a scientist named Heinrich Schleimann scoured the area. At last he hit pay dirt. Schliemann found not one city, but *nine* — each built over the ruins of the last one.

Most scholars agree that Troy VII — the seventh city from the top of the pile — was probably the city that Homer was talking about (although lately, Troy VI is getting a lot of votes!). Troy VII shows signs of having been under attack for a long time. The city had larger-than-usual amounts of stored provisions buried under house floors. And houses were built defensively, clustered together away from the city walls. Most important, it had been deliberately burned to the ground.

But the study of Troy has had its problems. Turkey has been at war many times, making archaeological digs there impossible. Also, funding has come and gone over the years.

Now, however, an international team of scientists is gearing up for a new, 20-year study of the site. This study is headed by Manfred Korfmann, who has permission from the Turkish government to work there. The funding is provided by carmaker Daimler-Benz.

Excavation of Troy has come a long way from the days of the pickax. Korfmann's group is using a specially designed earth mover called the Archäolog. It is also using the help of computers. By feeding computers information, Korfmann hopes to reconstruct what the site may have looked like thousands of years ago.

The best news is that, while Korfmann and his fellow scientists uncover Troy, they will also be setting up an open-air museum. Perhaps someday you will walk down the streets of Homer's Troy — a city once considered only a legend!

Underwater Cities

Recently, a new type of archaeology has come into its own, thanks to famous ocean explorer Jacques Cousteau. His invention of the aqualung in the 1940s freed people to explore under water without having to wear a heavy diving suit.

Usually people explore sunken wrecks, important sources of information about people of all times. But sometimes they find old harbors and even ancient cities that sank out of site thousands of years ago.

Two thousand years ago, a Jewish historian named Flavius Josephus wrote about a great harbor on the coast of what is now Israel. It was built by King Herod, at the edge of the city of Caesaria. Josephus described this port as a marvel of advanced engineering in his day.

According to Josephus, the harbor was ringed with a huge wall so sturdy that not even the heaviest storm could send in waves. Ships could moor and their cargo was safe, no matter what the weather was like. Arches built on the walls themselves housed mariners. The wall had watchtowers on it, and two tall towers at the opening where ships came in. This opening was also lined with immense statues called "Colossi," which stood on huge pillars.

For many years scholars read what Josephus had written and wondered what he was talking about. There was no port where Josephus had said it had been. So, like Pompeii, the port at Caesaria became a lost, legendary place.

Then, about 25 years ago, underwater archaeologists located the ancient port. It had sunk under the ocean, and was some distance off the coast of the city of Haifa. The harbor walls had fallen down, but their outline was clearly visible. The harbor of Caesaria, once lost, had been found.

Another sunken marvel that was once a legend has been located in India. Just as Homer's *Iliad* spoke about the ancient Western world, the *Mahabarata* is an epic poem that tells about India's ancient times.

One of its many stories tells of the beautiful capital city of the Hindu god Krishna. This city was supposedly built on a coast in India about 3,500 years ago. But only thirty-six years after the Golden City of Krishna was built, the sea level rose and covered it forever.

Krishna knew things before they happened. So he evacuated his people before the city sank. All its inhabitants were safe, but the Golden City of Krishna was gone.

For years, archaeologists read about this place and doubted that it had ever existed. They believed that in the India of 3,500 years ago, people were too backward to have built a city so grand. Perhaps, they decided, the *Mahabarata* was making what was really a simple village into a city of legendary beauty.

Archaeologist S.R. Rao disagreed. He matched up what was known of early Indian history and what had been written in the *Mahabarata*. As a probable site for the city, he settled on an area just off the Arabian Sea, on the western tip of India. It is near the Indian town called Dwaraka.

He was so convincing in his research that the National Institute of Oceanography sent a ship and divers to investigate Rao's claims.

Almost immediately, divers found shapes not normally found underwater. They cleared away a thick growth of kelp and uncovered a fort wall that was later proved to be about 3,500 years old.

Since then, underwater archaeologists have uncovered streets, palaces, temples, fortifications, and docks. They have found so many artifacts of the people who once lived there, that they are worried about how to document all the pieces!

Krishna's capital city is no longer a legend. But not all questions have been answered. Scientists may never know what caused the sea level to rise and swallow this ancient city.

Camelot

Camelot, the capital city of King Arthur's time, has been a legend for almost 1,500 years. So far, no one has found it. But one woman, Norma Lorre Goodrich, feels that it's because we're looking in the wrong country!

It is generally agreed there was a great military leader in Britain around the year 500 A.D. He may or may not have been British. He may or may not have been a king. His name may or may not have been Arthur. But someone, scholars agree, lived and was strong enough to give his country years of peace at a time of great unrest.

A sculpture of King Arthur.

For centuries, scholars have looked long and hard for Arthur's legendary city and they have always come up empty-handed. The trouble, Ms. Goodrich argues, is that we've been looking in England for 1,500 years. She feels that we should be looking in Scotland, instead!

Ms. Goodrich is not an archaeologist. She is a professor who has made a lifetime study of early stories about King Arthur and his world. She has studied descriptions of geography in early Arthurian stories. For instance, she noted when a character traveled west or east, whether they crossed a bridge or climbed a mountain, and how long it took them to complete their journey.

Her conclusions are much too complicated to explain in these pages. But she has pinpointed the region of the "Firth of Forth" as the probable site for Arthur's kingdom. Several descriptions match closely with this area's geography.

It is narrow, so both east and west coasts could be defended quickly from invaders. It is a traditional area of powerful rulers (Edinburgh, the capital of Scotland, is here). And instead of being inhabited by pagan tribes of Picts, this particular area was Christian during Arthur's time.

Is she correct? Will Arthur's legendary city be found, just as Troy and the port at Caesaria and the Golden City of Krishna have been? Only time will tell!

4
Places of Mystery

Certain places on Earth have more than their share of mystery about them. Stonehenge in England is one of these places.

Stonehenge is situated in Southwest England. It sits on Salisbury Plain, a lovely open pasture where cows and sheep have grazed for as long as people have lived in England. But as one's gaze rolls over the scene, suddenly it looks as though huge rocks are growing out of the ground instead of trees!

These rectangular rocks are standing straight up. They weigh anywhere between 5 and 45 tons each. They face one another in a circular pattern. It's like a giant petrified merry-go-round.

The standing rocks have equally huge rectangular rocks lying on top of them. When these lintel stones lie on top of two standing stones, it looks like a door. But it's a door for giants!

In fact, Stonehenge was known as "Giant's Dance" in olden times.

Obviously some group of people put these enormous boulders there, carved them into shape, and placed them where they stand today. But who? And why? And how did they do what they did?

At one time, people believed that Merlin the magician built Stonehenge during the time of King Arthur. He used magic to put the rocks in place. At another time, Stonehenge was believed to be Merlin's burial place. Many people believed that Stonehenge was a gathering place on full-moon nights for "little people" such as fairies and leprechauns. Others believed it to be a sacred altar for Druids, an ancient Briton religious group. Recently, some people have felt that Stonehenge wasn't built for people on the ground. It was meant to be seen from above, by alien visitors who came to Earth in ancient times.

Archaeologists have studied Stonehenge carefully. And they have answered a few of the old questions, such as how Stonehenge's stones got there and how it was built.

Stonehenge was not built all at once, but in stages. In 2800 B.C. it began as a simple circle of earth, with a large uncarved boulder near the opening of the circle.

Over the next 800 years, Stonehenge gradually got its stones. There are two types of stones at Stonehenge. The first are bluestones, which weigh up to 5 tons apiece. The second are stones in the Sarsen Circle that can weigh up to 45 tons!

None of these stones can be found in Salisbury Plain. They had to be transported from other places. One likely spot is Milford Haven, about 20 miles away. Another is southwest Wales, which is farther away.

How did the stones get to Salisbury Plain? And how were the stones raised to stand upright?

The stones were cut from quarries in Milford Haven and Wales. Then they were floated down a system of rivers and streams on a string of tied-together canoes. When each stone got to the plain, it had to be rolled on timber "wheels" or pulled on sledlike structures to its future spot.

Stonehenge, or "Giant's Dance," as it was known in olden times.

Once the stones were at the site, they had to be carved into a rectangular shape of the proper size. Then each boulder was roped, put into position, and pulled so that it slid into a pre-dug hole and stood upright.

Scientists believe that the lintel stones were raised by a series of ever-higher wooden platforms. The huge boulder would be pulled from one platform to the next, higher one. The last platform would be even with the top of the upright stones. Then the lintel stone would be pulled from the last platform onto the standing stones.

Transporting these stones was no picnic. There were 82 stones in all. The larger ones would have taken over 1,000 people to move one stone.

Scientists believe that Stonehenge was never actually "finished." It was simply added to, taken from, and re-arranged for several thousand years!

To this day, nobody knows what Stonehenge's actual purpose was. But its arrangement of stones seems to be astronomical.

Shafts of sunlight (or moonlight) hit certain stones at certain times of the year, such as midsummer or midwinter. Stonehenge may have been a calendar. It told ancient people when seasons were about to change or when it was time for important religious events.

Over the centuries many stones have fallen or broken. But even without all of its stones, Stonehenge has an unbeatable air of mystery about it. People have always come to look at it. And they always will.

Easter Island

Easter Island is a tiny bit of land in the Pacific Ocean. It is almost 2,500 miles off the coast of Chile, South America.

The people of Easter Island are Polynesian. But this is no tropical island paradise. This island is covered with tough grasses, not lush jungle growth. It is windy and lonely looking. But then, Easter Island should look lonely — in only 100 years or so, its entire population was nearly wiped out. The Easter Island language, social culture, and religion were lost forever.

Early European explorers found Easter Island full of natives. But clashes between natives and explorers ended up with natives losing. Later, hundreds of natives were taken from their homes to be sold on the slave markets. And finally, the European disease of smallpox finished off all but a few of the remaining natives.

From thousands, the native population was reduced to a little over 400 by the 1860s. These few were converted to Christianity. They were taught European languages and customs. Soon they had lost all ties with their own history.

But Easter Island's mysterious ancestors left something behind that insures that they will always be remembered. They sculpted enormous stones into the shape of monstrously huge people, and 600 of these stones still dot the island.

It's no mystery where the rock came from. A quarry on the island still shows 53 unfinished statues, which were being carved out of solid rock.

The statues that have been finished are very impressive-looking. They are anywhere from 11 to 18 feet tall and weigh about 20 tons each. Their huge heads take up almost half of the statue's length. They are placed upright on platforms, so that they look out to sea. Sometimes their flatly carved heads are topped with red stone "caps" almost as tall as the head under it.

Stone carvings at Easter Island.

The statues' expressions are stern. They seem to be staring into eternity, waiting for something. Some of the statues are still upright. Some have fallen over or broken. Some are buried in sand drifts up to their necks. And still others lean crazily to one side, as if unwilling to fall down.

But no matter what their position, Easter Island's statues are a source of many questions and few answers. Why were they carved? What do they mean? Are they meant to be gods? Do they represent long-dead ancestors? Were they put up to frighten would-be invaders who might look from their ships and think that Easter Island was a place inhabited by giants? Or do the statues represent war victories of some sort?

We may never know. And the Easter Island statues are not talking. They just stare toward the sea, waiting for — something.

Nazca, Peru

The Nazca plain is in the southwestern section of Peru, in South America. It is only 38 miles inland from the Pacific Ocean.

When you stand on the ground there, the area looks harsh, dry, and rocky. Every so often, you might see small mounds of stones that look as if someone had deliberately put them there. But it's not mysterious-looking. The Nazca plain just looks like a barren area with little piles of rocks!

In an airplane, though, the Nazca plain looks

quite different. Seen from above, you might see dozens of perfectly straight lines that look as if they had been drawn with a ruler. You might also see triangles, rectangles, or spirals. Or you might see, as though drawn on a giant blackboard, a monkey, a spider, a whale, a human hand, or a bird!

Now the Nazca plain is full of mysteries! Who made these lines and pictures? Why did they do it? Since they cannot be seen from the ground, whose attention were they supposed to have gotten?

Western civilization did not know about the Nazca lines until after the invention of the airplane. Their discovery was startling. Pilots, especially, looked at the rock-lined rectangles and realized that they looked for all the world like landing fields.

The thought of ancient, secret landing fields started wild theories about the lines. Some theories sound like science fiction stories.

One theory was that the "airfields" were built for "pilots" from the lost continent of Atlantis. When Atlantis sank, the airfields were of no further use. They were left as they were, to be found thousands of years later.

Another theory said that the "landing strips" were for UFOs. According to this theory, aliens landed on Earth in prehistoric times. They were friendly to our primitive ancestors. In fact, they may have taught early humans about the use of fire, or how to domesticate animals.

According to the theory, during their stay the aliens would be on their main ship most of the time. But sometimes they would shuttle to Earth's surface. The Nazca lines made it easy for the aliens to know where to land. The landing strip rectangles, the straight lines, and the animal pictures were for them to see — from the air.

These sensational theories brought the Nazca lines to the world's attention. From the 1970s on, people have been descending on Nazca to see the "ancient landing fields." (There really *is* an airfield in the area today — it is for planes bringing tourists!)

Scientists now have less sensational ideas. They know that humans lived in the area as far back as 12,000 years. But they feel that the lines, rectangles, and pictures were used for ritual rites or dances. The animal drawings may have represented different clans or tribes — the monkey clan, or the spider clan. The ancient peoples may have been trying to catch the attention of their gods.

One person has been studying and charting the Nazca lines long before they became famous. She is German mathematician Maria Reiche. The mathematical precision of the lines first attracted her attention in 1946.

Reiche has her own theory, based on her calculations. The Nazca lines are, she says, an astronomical chart. The animal figures may be clan figures for ancient gods. But the lines show movements of sun, stars, and planets over many years.

Scientists tried to test Reiche's theory by computer. They fed information about a section of lines into the computer. Then the computer matched this with positions of key stars as they would have appeared in the Peruvian sky thousands of years ago. The computer did not find a significant match.

Reiche says that the scientists did not have all of the data she has amassed. On the other hand, she is not willing to share her hard work with just anybody. Fortunately an astronomer from Chicago named Phyllis Pitluga has gained Reiche's trust. Reiche *will* share her data with Pitluga, and the latter will publish Reiche's theory when it is ready.

In the meantime, the Nazca plain continues to be one of the Earth's most mysterious places. And the Nazca lines continue to raise more questions than they may ever answer.

Angkor Wat

Angkor Wat is the name of a temple in the ancient abandoned city of Angkor. It is one of the world's most mysterious places. It is also in one of its most dangerous places — the jungles of war-torn Cambodia.

The Western world learned about Angkor from French naturalist Henry Mouhot, who visited and wrote about this exotic Eastern ghost town in the

1860s. His writings captured popular imagination worldwide.

In the late 1800s, French scientists arrived and tried to free some of Angkor's monuments from the jungle growth covering them. The efforts went on for years. But after World War II, the French were expelled from Cambodia. Since then, one war after another has kept Angkor isolated from further study and restoration.

In its heyday, the beautiful city of Angkor was far from being isolated. In fact, it was once a center of civilization.

Angkor was the capital city of the powerful Khmer people, who ruled the area between 800 and 1400 A.D. The Khmer were an extremely advanced people. For example, their system of flood control and irrigation, and of careful land management, gave the people *four* crop harvests a year. That's much more food than is grown today in the same area!

The city of Angkor is three times the size of Manhattan. Angkor Wat is one of the finest buildings in the city. Its name means "temple of the capital." Begun in the 1100s, Angkor Wat's construction took thousands of workmen 30 years to build.

Angkor was built with the Hindu religion in mind, although both Hinduism and Buddhism were practiced in the ancient city of Angkor. Angkor Wat's shape is supposed to represent the moun--

tain on which Hindu gods and goddesses live. Earth's land and water are represented by the temple's outer wall and moat.

Like other buildings in Angkor, Angkor Wat is covered with statues and hundreds of bas-relief sculptures on its walls. These tell stories of Hindu gods, goddesses, and humans. Bas-relief is a type of sculpture in which figures bulge out from the flat rock on which they are carved. The carvings in Angkor are so "active" that it sometimes seems as though the walls are alive. People allowed to visit Angkor Wat have often remarked that it is

The city of Angkor Wat.

very eerie to be surrounded with such liveliness in such an abandoned area.

The Khmer civilization declined and finally fell apart around the 1400s. The country was taken over by Thai peoples and the new capital became Phnom Penh. The empty city of Angkor was soon covered in lush jungle vegetation.

Most of the world forgot about Angkor and Angkor Wat. But some people remembered the building, Angkor Wat, as a very holy place. Despite the fact that it was built as a Hindu chapel, over the centuries it became known as a Buddhist shrine.

Reaching this place of mystery was dangerous, so a pilgrimage to Angkor Wat was an act of extreme devotion. Still, for hundreds of years, individuals made the pilgrimage. They prayed to Buddha and left offerings at Angkor Wat. Usually these offerings were statues of Buddha. Over the centuries, thousands of them collected in Angkor Wat's rooms.

In recent years Angkor Wat has not been visited often. Cambodia has been the scene of brutal war for decades. Some monuments, including Angkor Wat, show bullet holes and mortar damage. But recently both Indians and Cambodians have realized Angkor's importance to their histories. Indians recognize it as an important area of Hinduism. And it is important to Cambodians as part of their ancestral heritage. So, a joint effort to clear and restore at least some of the more important temples has begun.

Perhaps someday Angkor Wat will shine again, and Angkor's streets will be filled with people once more.

5
Earth on the Move

Earth doesn't have one smooth surface, like the outside of a balloon. It's more like a bunch of mosaic chips set on oil. Very slowly, the chips move away from one another, bump into one another, and slide under or over one another.

Scientists call these moving chips of land "tectonic plates." Instead of sliding on oil, tectonic plates slide over the intensely hot, liquid core of the earth. These plates are found all over the world. There are dozens of them, all traveling in various directions.

The entire Pacific Ocean is on one tectonic plate. The borders of the Pacific plate form a huge circle, from the bottom of South America up the western borders of South and North America, over to Asia, and back down to the eastern coast of Australia.

In some places, the Pacific plate is pulling the plate next to it underneath, to the bottom of the Pacific Ocean. In several million years it may pull the west coast of America under the Pacific plate and back into the center of the earth's core.

Borders between plates are known as rifts or ridges. These borders rub against one another, causing much volcanic and earthquake action. The borders of the Pacific plate are known as the Ring of Fire because of all the volcanic activity along the plate's edges. This volcanic activity was responsible for the formation of the Hawaiian islands and the islands that make up Japan.

The Atlantic Ocean is split in half by two plates. The border between these plates is known as the mid-Atlantic rift. It cuts between North and South America on one side, and Europe and Africa on the other.

The mid-Atlantic rift is not pulling one plate under another, like parts of the Pacific plate. Instead, it is pushing two giant plates apart. Liquid from the earth's center is oozing out and cooling in the Atlantic Ocean depths. The new earth pushes the old earth to either side. This rift pushed Europe and North America apart. And it is why South America and Africa look like two halves of the same puzzle.

Tectonic plate movement is responsible for the breakup of Earth's one original continent into the several we live on now. That "mother ship" of continents was Pangea.

Pangea
Two hundred million years ago there was one

continent. Scientists call it Pangea. It was roughly C-shaped. The top part of the C was North America, northern Europe and Asia, and the Arctic. The middle part of the C was Africa and South America. The bottom part of the C was made up of what is now Antarctica, Australia, and India.

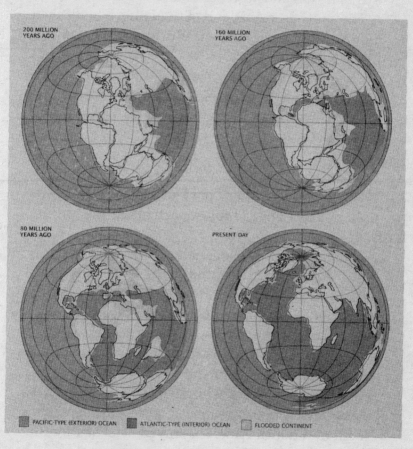

Continental drift over the ages.

Then, thanks largely to the Atlantic rift pushing in one direction and the Pacific plates pulling in another, Pangea began to break up. The top of the horseshoe stayed near the North Pole, but spread out. North America was on one side of Earth and Eurasia was on the other side.

The southeast Asia end of the Pangea horseshoe didn't move apart so much. But it did move down, like a long tail.

The rest of Pangea broke off dramatically, forming a second maxi-continent. This happened about 160 million years ago. Scientists call this Gondwanaland.

Gondwanaland

Gondwanaland was part of Pangea that was pulled off as Pangea broke apart, about 160 million years ago.

Gondwanaland was made up of what is now South America, Africa, India, the Near East, Antarctica, and Australia. It lasted 60 million years or more before it, too, began to break up.

Eventually the forces of the Atlantic, Pacific, and other plates broke this vast continent into other, smaller ones. In the words of Australians, the continents "went walkabout."

Africa and South America were pushed apart. North and South America stayed attached by the slender thread of Central America.

But Africa continued moving up and out, until

it slammed against Europe and Asia. Part of Africa wedged itself into Asia and became the Arab countries. Another chunk of Gondwanaland broke off and rammed itself into southern Asia to become India.

Meanwhile, the bottom of Gondwanaland broke off to become Antarctica. Another piece kept moving to become Australia!

Because of the way Australia moved, it has become a living museum of the last living Gondwanaland plants and animals.

Most of the "walkabout" continents are connected to one another. So even though their climates and locales changed drastically from what they had been as Gondwanaland, plants and animal life could still travel from one continent to another. Eventually they evolved into the plants and animals we know now.

The exception was Australia. Australia was never connected with other land masses as it broke away from Gondwanaland. So, like an ark, it moved with all its animal and plant life intact.

Australian plants and animals aren't *exactly* like the fossils found in Gondwanian times. But they are direct descendants of those in Gondwanaland, found nowhere else on Earth.

For instance, in Gondwanian times, marsupials were a dominant type of mammal life. Marsupial animals raise their young in a pouch. Fossils found in Australia show that some early mammals were marsupials first, before they began giving birth to fully developed young. Scientists have even found the fossil of a marsupial lion!

As Gondwanaland broke up, marsupial animals were gradually replaced by placental mammals who developed their unborn babies inside their bodies instead of inside a pouch. In most countries, the only marsupial animal left is the opossum.

On Australia, marsupials had no competition from newer forms of mammals. So they kept on living to the present day. Now Australia is famous for its marsupials, especially the kangaroo and the koala bear.

Recently, scientists have found fossils of marsupial life from old Gondwanaland so unusual that they are called "Thingodonta." That's because scientists don't know what to call them!

Today

Earth's surface hasn't stopped moving just because we don't feel it! Various tectonic plates are pushing and pulling countries together and apart every minute of every day.

We know that our continents are drifting. But where are they going? Satellites help scientists measure the movement of our present continents. By measuring the exact position of continents each year, scientists hope to get an idea of where different countries are headed!

6
Locations Coming Up and Going Down

The earth's surface doesn't only move north, south, east, and west. If we could speed up time, our "solid Earth" would also be going up and down like a bowl of boiling oatmeal!

Bit by bit, without our noticing, mountains are pushed up. Thin layers of Earth collapse into hollow areas underneath. As we have already seen, the Atacama Desert rose straight up from the Pacific Ocean. And the ancient city of Krishna, once on dry land, now lies under water.

Of course, sometimes an event happens with frightening rapidity. Whole areas disappear during earthquakes. And once in a while, something new appears. The island of Surtsey is one of the new areas.

Surtsey
Surtsey was born on November 14, 1963. It is 20 miles south of Iceland. When local fishermen saw the first smoke on the ocean's surface they

thought a ship was burning. But this was no ship — it was an underwater volcano erupting.

The volcanic eruption started from 380 feet under the ocean. When red-hot lava hit the icy Atlantic, it sent up steam four miles high, and hardened into rock much more quickly than it would have on land.

In 16 days the volcano's fury had not only broken the ocean's surface, it had created an island 1,110 yards long. For months, Surtsey grew an acre a day. By March, the island was a mile square. At present, it is almost two miles square.

Scientists were ecstatic. For them, it was like being present at the beginning of the world. From the first moment they knew about the volcano, scientists watched, measured, and probed. They knew that by witnessing the birth of this island, they would know more about other islands' formations. Also, scientists wanted to know when and how plant and animal life gets to Earth's newest places.

The first seven people who tried to land on Surtsey were almost killed by a shower of pumice and ash. (This was the same thing that had buried the citizens of Pompeii.)

For months, visiting the new island was a calculated risk. Things might be quiet, but visitors might also find themselves suddenly running from a barrage of lava chunks hurled at them like cannonballs.

When the island was settled in and became permanent after about 1½ years, scientist Sturla Fridricksson settled in, too. He has been studying Surtsey's progress for over 25 years now. Surtsey has come a long way from being a black, barren spot on the ocean. It now has 25 species of plants. Six types of seabirds nest there. Perhaps someday a few people might take residence on Surtsey, just as they did on a string of volcanic islands in the Pacific now known as Hawaii.

Venice, Italy

Venice, Italy, is built on 118 tiny islands, just off the coast of Italy. It is surrounded by the Adriatic Sea, connected to the mainland by a bridge and a highway.

The city has always been famous. It became a rich trading port and a center of culture from the 1200s to the 1400s. At that time the city was known as the "Queen of the Sea."

Many rich and powerful people built beautiful houses, filling them with now-priceless paintings and sculptures. The city's main church is St. Mark's, famous the world over for its incredible beauty. Some of the world's great church music was written to be performed in St. Mark's.

Venice is also where gondoliers ferry people from place to place in gondola boats, through a complicated system of canals. It is the only way to get around in a city built on 118 islands! The gondoliers and their gondolas are famous the world over as a symbol of Italy. In any Italian restaurant, chances are there will be a picture or painting of a gondola being poled along a canal.

Today, Venice is still a big shipping center. But it is also a huge tourist attraction. Thousands of people descend on Venice every year to ride in a gondola and to feed the pigeons in St. Mark's square. It seems a miracle that this beautiful place exists where it does. The whole city seems to be sitting right on the water.

A "street" in Venice, Italy.

Only one thing is wrong with this picture. Venice is sinking at a rate that has increased from 4 inches every hundred years to 9 inches in this century alone! That may not sound like much but, in Marco Polo's time, 700 years ago, Venice was at least 3 feet higher.

Venetians have long noticed that winter floods have become worse and more frequent. But November 4, 1966, was a clear warning of things to come. That year the tide rose six feet over its usual level. St. Mark's was flooded. Homes, hotels, shops, and museums still show high-water marks from that awful time. You have to look up to see those marks.

Since then, floods have been less severe, but more frequent. Not only is Venice going down, but the oceans are rising! Worldwide global warming is melting long frozen ice and raising the sea level all over the world. The 1966 flood made Venice realize that it was living on borrowed time.

What to do with a sinking city? Abandon it? Raise it? Learn to live with it?

The city of Venice instead decided to do something about the Adriatic Sea which surrounds it. After 20 years of planning, city leaders think they may be able to control some flooding. The idea is to construct an underwater "city wall," which can be lowered in good times and raised in flood times.

A test section is in place now. It looks roughly like a big door hinge. And that's the way it works.

One side of the "hinge" is a concrete base lying on the sea bed, holding everything down. The other side is the "wall" section, which will be raised and lowered. A pipe runs between these two sections.

The moving part of the wall has a heavy duty "mattress" connected to it. The pipe runs air into the mattress, which *floats* the movable part of the wall into place. When the wall reaches a certain angle, it locks into place and stays there until the danger is over. Then the mattress is deflated, and the hinge shuts again.

The movable Venetian wall is simple and workable. But it is not cheap! It will cost at least $2.6 billion to build. Venice hopes to have it built and working by 1996.

Will Venice's new seawall solve all its flooding problems? No, say engineers. To do that, the wall would have to be up at least 40 times a year. That would interrupt shipping, and would create a pollution problem for the city of Venice.

So far, they've decided that Venice can live with ankle-deep water in less than a tenth of the city. If flooding is worse than that, they will lift the wall. This way the "wall" will only have to go up three or four times a year.

Sinkholes

How would you like to go into your backyard and find out that you don't have a backyard any more? Instead, you have a huge hole that appeared overnight! Your problem is a sinkhole.

Sometimes underground streams carve holes into soft rock such as limestone. The underground holes may become caves, such as the ones described in Chapter 1. But if the layer of soil above is thin, it may collapse to become a sinkhole. Also, when humans take water out of underground sources faster than it can fill up again, man-made sinkholes may occur.

Some places are known for their sinkholes. As you cross a certain lake in South Australia, the bottom suddenly drops out to reveal a sinkhole famous for the amazing clarity of its water. Divers swimming in this sinkhole say it is like taking a space walk. Another said it is like flying.

Florida has many sinkholes. One of them, Warm Mineral Springs, found near Venice, Florida, is famous to health enthusiasts who like to soak in its mineral water. It is also famous to archaeologists who dive deep into the same sinkhole and find artifacts that go all the way back to the Ice Age.

Apparently, people have always thrown things into this sinkhole. Early inhabitants threw in their dead, and the bones of animals they ate. Archaeologists have been unearthing skulls of the earliest Americans, and skeletons of such animals as saber-toothed tigers. Later artifacts, such as an aluminum chair, are being left for scientists of the future to bring up!

Lakeland, Georgia, had a sinkhole encounter of the worst kind a few years ago. Plans to change a parking lot into a basketball court changed fast when nature gave them an 80-foot round, 30-foot deep hole instead. Undaunted city officials tried to think of what they could do with an asphalt-covered hole. They connected it to a nearby pond and turned it into a fishing area!

This house was the victim of a sinkhole in Florida.

7
Changing Earth

Have you ever looked at a photo of yourself from a year ago? It's usually a shock to see how much you've changed! But day by day, it didn't seem as though anything much had happened.

Earth is something like that. We don't see a mountain range one day and nothing the next. But over thousands — or even millions — of years, places become radically different.

Fish in the Desert

The Sahara Desert, in Northern Africa, is famous for its dryness. In some areas, this desert is so dry that the only thing moving in it is sand.

But things weren't always this way. Scientists have known for a long time that the Sahara had once been wetter. Salt flats from evaporated salt water, for instance, show where large lakes once stood. But it wasn't until 1982 that they realized just *how* wet it may have been.

In 1982, scientists were looking over radar pho-

65

tos taken from the space shuttle *Columbia*. The pictures of the Sahara desert look mysteriously webbed, as though the desert were crisscrossed with channels. Because of the nature of the photos, scientists realized that these channels were just under the sand.

In 1984, the U.S. Geological Survey sent researchers into the area to see what these strange markings might be. They concluded that the markings were channels of ancient rivers and streams. The Sahara, at various times, was *full* of them!

Apparently water has been turning off and on over the eras like a Sahara faucet. There have been dry times when rivers broke up into watering holes. But there have been wet times when annual rainfall averaged 20 inches a year. (Annual rainfall nowadays is under 5 inches a year.) This has been going on for from 20 million years ago to about 4,000 years ago.

After the river channels had been mapped, archaeologists located some of them and dug there. They hit ancient pay dirt right away. Hand axes and other artifacts they found indicated that people lived there from about 200,000 years ago. In other places, they found evidence that people lived in these areas as lately as 4,000 years ago.

But how do scientists know for sure that these are water channels? Paleontologists dug where the channels were, and located fossils of mammals, birds, reptiles, amphibians, and — fish.

In one area they found fossils of deep-water fish. That meant that there had to be a way for the fish to get from a deep sea to the spot in which they were found. The system of river channels, they believe, once connected the Sahara to the Nile Valley.

Scientists want to know much more about the water-soaked Sahara of the past. But they must wait until another set of radar photos is taken from another space shuttle. It should happen some time after 1991.

Lions in Alaska

The last Ice Age took place about one and a half million years ago. It is known as the Pleistocene Era. At that time, Canada and northern North America were covered with sheets of ice.

That is the usual picture of the Ice Age, right? Vast sheets of ice covering everything from the North Pole to Minnesota! But that isn't the whole story.

There was a grassy, treeless plain, which was actually above the ice sheets. This plain was located in what is now the Canadian Yukon and northern Alaska. The unusual area is known as Mammoth Steppe, named after the woolly mammoths that once roamed there.

Mammoth Steppe's size and shape varied according to what the surrounding ice was doing.

Woolly mammoths and saber-toothed tigers battled 12,000 years ago.

When the ice expanded into steppe territory, Mammoth Steppe shrank. Sometimes, the ice froze up enough water to dry out a path between Mammoth Steppe and Asia. That is why Siberia and Alaska show the same animal groups for the same years.

Mammoth Steppe wasn't a warm, comfy oasis! Life was pretty tough. But it was possible for animals to live there, which they could not do in the ice-covered areas.

Since Mammoth Steppe was a grassland, it was full of grazing animals. Besides the woolly mammoths, there were ancient bison, antelopes, horses, donkeys, reindeer, woolly rhinos, sheep, deer, and camels. But these plant eaters were hunted by meat-eating saber-toothed cats, cheetahs, wolves, and lions.

Lions in the Yukon? It seems impossible to us that lions once hunted antelope above the Arctic Circle. But many fossils from the Pleistocene Era prove they were there. And the lions of that time were like the African lions of today, except that the males didn't have big manes.

Mammoth Steppe life went on for over a million years. But its climate began changing around 12,000 years ago. It became wetter and colder, bringing deep snows. Eventually the animals of Mammoth Steppe moved or died out.

The area which was once Mammoth Steppe is now very different. The ground never thaws out. There are no grasslands within a thousand miles of the place where lions once stalked camels and bison. Only small animals such as lemmings live in the area now.

Collision Course with Destiny

It has long been obvious to scientists that something big happened around 66 million years ago. This was a time between two of Earth's big periods — the Cretaceous and the Tertiary. It marks the end of the dinosaurs and the beginnings of the world as we know it now.

But what happened? What triggered the end of a species that had ruled Earth for at least 75 million years? Would you believe a meteorite with a diameter of 10 miles crashing into Earth at 45,000 miles per hour?

Dinosaurs from the Late Cretaceous Period.

A team of four scientists headed by geologist Dr. Alvarez believes just that, from studying soil layers in a northern Italian town.

Geologists can tell a lot about long-ago Earth by studying ancient soil layers. In 1985, the Alvarez group found that soil from 66 million years ago was full of soot and a usually rare element called iridium.

The element iridium is so rare on Earth that it is measured in parts per trillion. The only other place where so much is usually found is at meteorite impact sites. That's because iridium is brought in on the meteorite. And there was *lots* of iridium in the 66-million-year-old soot layer from Italy.

Alvarez' group began looking for iridium in the same "time zone" of rocks in other countries. So far, 95 concentrations of iridium have been found all over the world. They are always in the 66-million-year-ago layer of Earth.

If deposits from a meteorite are all over Earth in the same time zone, it must have filtered down from a gigantic worldwide cloud of dust and soot. And a meteorite impact big enough to raise this much dust must have made quite a bang.

All right, you say, so there was a big meteorite. So it slammed into Earth. So what?

Well — if you believe in this theory — then the meteorite and widely scattered bits from it hit the Earth burning. This started fires all over the place. It burned up a great deal of Earth. The thick smoke choked a lot of animals. It killed a lot of plants.

Smoke was so thick that it may have blocked out the sun worldwide. The climate may have gone from hot to freezing because the sun was blocked out. Or, some scientists believe, the smoke may have caused a gigantic greenhouse effect. This might have made the earth unbearably hot for many years — until the dust settled.

Whether they couldn't breathe, or whether they were too hot or too cold, dinosaurs were wiped out. So were many plant forms. There are even one-celled marine animals that were completely wiped out.

But wait — where is the meteor hole? A 10-mile crater would leave quite a dent! Scientists believe that over 66 million years, the "hole" is no longer around. It may have been pushed up into a mountain range. It may have been filled with volcanic lava or silt. Or it may have eroded until it can no longer be identified.

8
Windows to the Past

Isn't rummaging around Grandma's attic or basement a great way to learn about one's family? You may find old photos of parents or grandparents from when they were your age. You can try on old clothes, or maybe an old uniform. You might even get to look at your mom's or dad's report cards! Finding actual things from long ago brings the past alive in a way that no other experience can.

Earth has something in common with Grandma's attic. There are places where things from long ago can still be found. These things may be preserved bones from an animal long extinct, or an insect trapped inside million-year-old tree resin. It could even be the mummy of an ancient animal or human. But whatever we find makes Earth's past seem alive to us all.

A Fly in Amber
Paleontologists know about ancient animals

mainly by studying their preserved bones. These bones, reconstructed, give us an idea of what the animal once looked like.

But tiny insect bodies rot away long before they can be preserved. And even if insect parts are discovered, they cannot be reconstructed. So scientists end up knowing about how horses developed over millions of years, but not how ants or bees did.

Some insects, however, did get preserved. Ancient tree resin was bad luck for the bugs, but good luck for scientists!

Tree resin is very common in trees of today. It is usually found on conifers, such as pine or spruce trees. If you touch their trunks, you will find that the resin is very sticky. Some types of resin are made into varnish or even glue.

Ancient conifer trees had sticky resin on their trunks millions of years ago. Sometimes this resin dried out and hardened into a clear yellow-to-brown stone called amber.

Just as they do today, ants, flies, bees, and spiders sometimes got caught in the sticky resin. They died, covered in it. If that resin later hardened into amber, the insect inside would become perfectly preserved. The same thing happened to plant parts that got stuck in any sap that fell to the ground. If that sap turned into amber, the plants in the sap became perfectly preserved specimens.

Most amber is between 50 and 80 million years old. Some pieces are much older. And anything trapped inside that amber is as old as the amber itself!

Amber is commonly used for jewelry since it is a very pretty, clear stone. Scientists want amber for study, not for earrings! But they still must sometimes buy amber from jewelry dealers before it is sold and cut up for jewels. In 1985, the Smithsonian National Museum of Natural History got 5,000 amber pieces in just that way. Discoveries found in these stones are almost a miracle. One of the pieces contained a perfectly preserved 80-million-year-old stingerless bee!

Organisms trapped in amber are startlingly well preserved. Ants still have antennae. Flies have their wings. One 40-million-year-old fly was so well preserved that its abdomen cells could be studied.

Scientists have also found other rarities. Flower petals, leaves, and stems millions of years old are so perfectly preserved that their cell structure may be seen through a microscope. They once found an actual tuft of hair from a mammal that died 80 million years ago! Frogs and even lizards have been found preserved in amber.

But lately, scientists have been looking for something even rarer. They believe that air bubbles in a piece of amber may contain the actual atmosphere from 80 million years ago!

La Brea Tar Pits

Rancho La Brea has been dubbed by scientists as a gigantic fossil time capsule. Located at the edge of Los Angeles, there are a hundred or more ancient tar pits. These have yielded more than 565 different types of animals that lived here from as far back as 40,000 years ago.

At roughly the same time that lions were hunting woolly mammoths on Mammoth Steppe (Chapter 7), crude oil was bubbling up through cracks in La Brea's soil. Eventually the surface oil hardened into "ponds" of natural asphalt.

In hot weather, asphalt gets soft and sticky. If you have ever walked across a newly laid asphalt road, you know how sticky it can be!

Sometimes the ancient sticky asphalt got covered with dust and looked just like the surrounding ground. Or, if it became covered with rainwater, the asphalt looked like an innocent watering hole. But it wasn't. It was a Stone Age drama about to unfold.

The scene is a lovely spring day 25,000 years ago. An ancient mastodon (an early type of elephant) decides to wade in a pond it sees. But when it steps into the "pond," it finds that it cannot get back out. The animal struggles, but it is only trapped further. Sticky black asphalt holds it as strongly as flypaper holds insects.

The panicked animal looks up and sees its worst nightmare — wolves. They leap upon the struggling mastodon and rip out its throat. But now

*An American mastodon
unearthed from
the La Brea tar pits.*

they, too, are trapped and cannot get out.

The fresh meat of the mastodon brings scavengers and predators to the same spot. A saber-toothed tiger, an Ice Age lion, vultures, and hyenas all come for an easy meal — and all become trapped in the sticky tar.

Scenes such as this were played out over and over at La Brea. Eventually, an amazing number of animals became concentrated in certain spots where ancient asphalt pools once lay.

The tar pits were also discovered by ancient man who used its asphalt for themselves. Native Americans made glue and waterproofing material from it. Early Spanish explorers kept their fires burning with La Brea's tar, as far back as 1769.

But the tar pit's ancient bones lay undisturbed until its asphalt was "mined" for roads in the 1800s. At that time strange bones were found at La Brea. These bones were not from animals anyone had ever seen. The scientific community became interested. By the early 1900s, full-scale excavations were taking place.

The first excavations were crude by present standards. Now, better techniques for removing animal remains from the hardened asphalt have helped scientists recover bones of delicate animals not usually found elsewhere.

For instance, La Brea's tar pits have yielded more than 138 species of birds. Their tiny, hollow bones were coated and protected for thousands of years. But it was only after the late 1960s that the tinier bones could be separated from their tomb of hardened tar.

Nowadays scientists study everything from ancient songbirds and turkeys to now-extinct types of vultures and eagles. They have also found remains of frogs and toads whose last act was to hop into what they thought was a pond. Scientists have also found ancient turtles, ducks, and geese.

La Brea's deceptive tar pits fooled almost all

creatures — except humans. So far, only one set of human bones has been found in the asphalt pits. A 25-year-old, 4-foot-10-inch female, now known as "La Brea Woman," met her unfortunate end around 9,000 years ago.

You'd think with over a million ancient bones to study, scientists would be happy and busy. But they are looking for even smaller things now. As removal techniques improve, they are finding bits of wood, seeds, cones, and leaves, as well as ancient insect parts!

Meanwhile, La Brea continues to be one of Earth's best windows to the past.

Mummies

Wouldn't it be amazing to have a dinosaur, a woolly mammoth, or an ancient human walk right up to you from the past? Natural and man-made mummies are as close as modern people will ever get to having such an experience.

In two societies, mummies of humans were made on purpose. Both societies — ancient Egypt and ancient Chile — dried the bodies of their dead.

Egyptians covered the dried bodies with a kind of varnish to keep all moisture away. They wrapped the bodies in linen cloth, and closed them in tight-fitting mummy cases. Completed mummies were then set in one of many underground vaults in a necropolis, or "City of the Dead."

Chilean mummies were covered in an air-tight

covering of clay. A stick was run through the body, where the spinal cord was, to keep it standing. And the bodies were buried standing up as if at eternal attention.

Egyptian mummies can be anywhere from 1,500 years old to 4,000 years old. Once they were common, but over the centuries they have become rare. Scientists study the bodies to find out what people ate, the diseases they suffered from, and what their daily lives were like.

An Egyptian mummy.

Chilean mummies are much older. Some are as old as 8,000 years! Plus, there are so many mummies buried around Arica, Chile, that local residents consider them a nuisance. Every time they dig a garden or build a house, they have to clear out mummies the way most people clear out tree roots!

Scientists are just beginning to study Chilean mummies. They want to know what life was like for Native Americans of the area before Europeans arrived. Chilean mummies may provide answers that would otherwise have been shrouded in the past.

Natural mummies are formed in three ways. They are either dried out, frozen, or chemically preserved.

In 1908, fossil collector Charles Sternberg and his son George were in Wyoming looking for dinosaur bones. It was a good day. They had uncovered an excellent "duckbilled" dinosaur skeleton.

Then, as George later wrote: " . . . when I removed a rather large piece of sandstone rock from over the breast I found . . . a perfect impression of the skin beautifully preserved. . . . "

The Sternbergs had found the only dinosaur mummy to that date. Before that, no one had any idea what dinosaur skin might have looked like. The Sternberg's mummy now lies just as it was found, in New York City's American Museum of Natural History.

Since that time, skin has been found on other dinosaur mummies. Most of it is pebbly and hard, like the skin on a football. Some dinosaur mummies contain a last meal, so scientists can tell what those dinosaurs ate.

Frozen mummies are found in places that are very cold. Siberia, in the USSR, is such a place.

Woolly mammoths grazed Siberian grasslands 40,000 years ago — just as they did on the Mammoth Steppe in Alaska (Chapter 7). But the Siberian landscape is broken by gulches and ravines. Animals falling into these holes either escaped or starved.

Dima was an 8-month old woolly mammoth that had not even been weaned from its mother. One day Dima slipped into a gully and could not climb out. Its mother could not reach it. Dima grew thinner and thinner, finally eating dirt in a desperate attempt to live. But it died.

Because Dima was small, the little mammoth froze quickly. Predators could no more reach its body than its mother could. Dima's body was buried, first under ice and snow, and then under earth, which froze in layers over the body. The little mammoth lay where it died for 40,000 years.

In 1977, prospectors came to Siberia looking for gold. Instead of useless chopping, they shot jets of water at the frozen earth to thaw it out. Suddenly one man saw something too bizarre for words. It was an elephant!

"Dima," a baby woolly mammoth
frozen 40,000 years ago in Siberia,
next to a model of a fully grown mammoth.

The men reported what they had found. Scientists rushed to the spot. They were amazed to find a complete frozen mammoth mummy, untouched by time or by predators. It was Dima. Dima is now on display in the Leningrad Museum, as one of Earth's most amazing windows to the past.

Chemically preserved mummies may be said to have been "pickled." Something has kept oxygen and bacteria away from the body, preventing it from decomposing. Peat bogs in Denmark do the job unusually well.

In 1950, workers were in a Danish peat bog cutting squares of peat to burn in their heating fires. About seven feet down, they came upon a body. They thought it was the body of a recent murder victim, and called police. But the police knew that no recently buried body would have seven feet of soil over it.

The police called the university. Scientists set about digging the man out. Tollund man, as he came to be called, was perfectly preserved. He seemed to have been about 40 years old. His hair, eyebrows, and eyelashes were intact. There was even stubble on his chin. His features had not shrunk at all. Every line of his face suggested that he could open his eyes and speak at any second.

Tollund man wasn't wearing any clothing. But he had on a leather cap, and there was a noose around his neck. At first, people thought Tollund man had been a convicted criminal. But his gentle features belied the thought.

Finally, scientists decided that he had gone to his death willingly and peacefully. He was probably sacrificed to his gods for the good of his tribe.

Only Tollund man's head has been kept for posterity. It is on display in the Silkeborg Museum

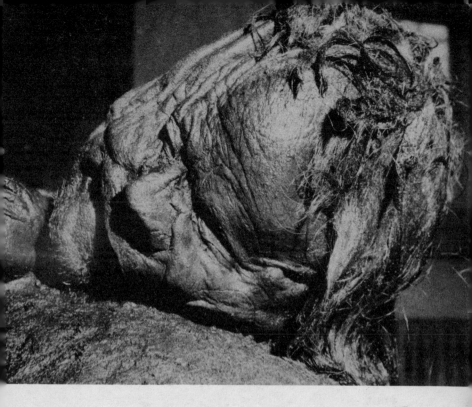

Hanged 2,000 years ago,
"Tollund Man" was almost perfectly preserved.

in Denmark. Tollund man is a startling look at the face of our human past. It causes us to realize that ancient people were real people, and had real lives.

As one scientist put it: "His handsome and fantastically well-preserved countenance makes a stronger and more convincing impression on us than the work of the most inspired sculptor could achieve."

9
What's in a Name?

People the world over have a passion to name the spot where they live. Some places have perfectly normal-sounding names. Other places are like the ones we found in the United States ZIP code book!

Here are a few places a person might want to visit:
Best, Texas; Clever, Missouri; Delight, Arkansas; Lovely, Kentucky; Luck, Wisconsin; Money, Mississippi; Pep, Texas; Romance, Arkansas; Sunshine, Louisiana; and Welcome, Maryland, Minnesota, or North Carolina!

But there are other places that don't sound as hospitable, such as:
Accident, Maryland; Bland, Virginia; Boring, Oregon; Camp Crook, South Dakota; Cheapside, Texas; Cut and Shoot, Texas; Dinkytown, Minnesota; Droop, West Virginia; Coward, South Car-

olina; Crummies, Kentucky; Defeated, or Difficult,
Tennessee; Eek, Arkansas; Loco, Oklahoma; Lost
City, or Odd, West Virginia; Remote, Oregon; Ordinary, Virginia; Peculiar, or Roach, Missouri; Vi-
per, Kentucky; Soso, Mississippi; or Why, Arizona!

Sometimes cities are in states that may come as
a surprise. For instance:
• Austin is in Texas and also in Arizona,
Colorado, Illinois, Indiana, Kentucky, Minnesota,
Nevada, and Pennsylvania.
• Boston is in Massachusetts and also in
Georgia, Indiana, Kentucky, Maine, New York,
Pennsylvania, Texas, and Virginia.
• Brooklyn is in New York and also in Alabama,
Connecticut, Indiana, Iowa, Kentucky, Michigan,
Mississippi, Ohio, Oregon, Pennsylvania, and
Wisconsin.
• Hollywood is in California and also in Florida,
Maryland, New Mexico, Oregon, South Carolina,
and Tennessee.
• Miami is in Florida and also in Arizona, In-
diana, Missouri, New Mexico, Oklahoma, Texas,
and West Virginia.
• Philadelphia is in Pennsylvania and also in
Mississippi, Missouri, New York, and Tennessee.

Many foreign locations seem to be wandering
around as well, such as:
• the city of Athens, which is in Greece and also

in Alabama, Georgia, Illinois, Indiana, Louisiana, Maine, Michigan, New York, Ohio, Pennsylvania, Tennessee, Texas, West Virginia, and Wisconsin.

• the city of Cairo, which is in Egypt and also in Georgia, Illinois, Missouri, Nebraska, New York, Ohio, and West Virginia.

• the city of London, which is in England and also in Arkansas, Kentucky, Minnesota, Ohio, Texas, and West Virginia.

• the city of Moscow, which is in Russia and also in Arkansas, Idaho, Iowa, Kansas, Michigan, Ohio, Pennsylvania, Tennessee, Texas, and Vermont.

• the city of Rome, which is in Italy and also in Georgia, Illinois, Indiana, Iowa, Mississippi, New York, Ohio, and Pennsylvania.

• the city of Warsaw, which is in Poland and also in Illinois, Indiana, Kentucky, Minnesota, Missouri, New York, North Carolina, Ohio, and Virginia.

• the country of Egypt, which is also in Arkansas, Kentucky, Mississippi, and Texas.

• the country of Cuba, which is also in Alabama, Illinois, Kansas, Missouri, New Mexico, New York, and Ohio.

• the country of Mexico, which is also in Indiana, Maine, Missouri, New York, and Pennsylvania.

• the country of Scotland, which is also in Arkansas, Connecticut, Georgia, Indiana, Maryland, Pennsylvania, and South Dakota.

• the country of Wales, which is also in Alaska, Maine, North Dakota, and Utah.

Some city names seem to indicate certain kinds of behavior. For instance:

Don't:

• bring a cat to Barking, Pennsylvania.
• chop a tree in Bad Axe, Michigan.
• say "Play it again, Sam" in Bogart, Georgia.
• be late in Early, Iowa or Texas.
• cheat in Fair Play, Missouri, Mississippi, or South Carolina.
• get dirty in Hygiene, Colorado.
• make fun of southpaws in Left Hand, West Virginia.
• stop in Start, Louisiana.
• lie in True, West Virginia.
• be a secretary in Typo, Kentucky — or
• make a typo in Secretary, Maryland!

10
Trivia!

Just as you have interesting stories about your life, Earth has some stories of its own.

For instance:

• Did you know that England has mysterious rings that appear in fields, sometimes near Stonehenge? Some are small and some are as big as a baseball diamond. They have come up from time to time, for no reason, in various fields. These round patterns can be seen best from the air, but they have been noticed for three hundred years. No one, not even the most cautious scientist, can prove that any human is making these circles. At this time, their appearance and disappearance is still a mystery.

• Did you know that the ocean abyss is full of man-made junk? The sea floor is very cold, so decomposition is slow. Scientists looking for deep-sea life have found instead such things as bottles, cans, a sink, fighter planes, a torpedoed ship from World War II, a thermometer, and a newspaper.

When a crippled deep-sea submersible, the Alvin, was brought back to the surface after a year, workers found a year-old lunch — a sandwich and an apple — that looked good enough to eat, if you like salt!

• Did you know that there are only two cities in the United States that begin with the letter "X"? They are both named Xenia — Xenia, Illinois, and Xenia, Ohio.

• Did you know that George Washington was an amateur spelunker, or cave explorer? He squeezed his 6'4" frame into caves all over Virginia. We know, because he left his signature carved into at least two caves. That means that George Washington may have also been America's most famous producer of graffiti!

• Did you know that the Hawaiian island of Kauai is not only the locality of the wettest spot on Earth, but it is also the location of "barking sands"? When sand on a certain beach is very dry and rubbed together, it produces a sound like a barking puppy. One early traveler said that when he ran his horse over dunes of this sand, the resulting sound was "loud enough to startle the horse."

• Did you know that the people in a Thai village where the Ban Chiang once lived, still make the same kind of pellet-shooting split string bows that have been found in graves over 3,000 years old?

• Did you know that Stonehenge is the scene of

riots every June 21? That is the date of the summer solstice, when the day is the longest day of the year. It was a holy time to Druids. Some people in England want to greet the solstice sun at Stonehenge, as they believe their ancestors did. But Stonehenge is now a tourist attraction. It is closed at dawn, and people are supposed to get there only through an underground tunnel. Police and "worshippers" clash every year. Many arrests are made, and sometimes people on both sides are hurt.